BEFORE YOU MET ME

AGATHA SICIL

RUNNING
Wild
PRESS

CONTENTS

"The hardest thing about the truth is finding it within yourself."

To my therapist: thank you for giving me the space to write my story.
To my mom, my sister, my great aunt, and the rest of my family: I'm sorry. I still am. Thank you for sticking by me and my side of the story.

BEFORE YOU MET ME, by Agatha Sicil

Text Copyright © 2023 Held by the author

Published in North America and Europe by Running Wild Press. Visit Running Wild Press at www.runningwildpress.com Educators, librarians, book clubs (as well as the eternally curious), go to ww.runningwildpress.com for teaching tools.

ISBN (pbk) 978-1-955062-69-5

ISBN (ebook) 978-1-955062-70-1

June 1, 99

Dearest Nicole,
                 Grandma
loves you very much, hope
you are doing well in school
school would soon be over,
and you would have a nice
long summer take good care
of yourself and enjoy your
summer I am sorry I won't
be able to see you in the
summer but if I hit the
Lotto I will send a plane
ticket for you first class
if only for a week (smile)
get what you need with the money
and call me when you
recived it, give Daniella $10.00
I love you, stay well and
write me soon, there is
a house on the corner before
you turn in my street

1

right on the corner
by the stop sign.
There is another one
coming up the block
on the same side with
me. thats the latest news

love you Always

your Grandma

JUNE 1, 1999

Missing
The blacktop gleamed across the once-desolate road.
It was a typical hot summer day.
Sun
scorching
streets
spent.
Florida temps can be a killer.
Literally.
The housing market was booming.
A once-desolate area.
Many houses are being built
"right on the corner,
by the stop sign."
A red octagon has so much power.
But over whom?
You?
Me?
No.
Them.
Summers were spent in northeast Florida.
Pool swimming.
Disney visiting.
Alligator hunting.
Bible reading.
Crying at night.
I want my mom.
Why did she have to send me away every summer?
First time I flew, I was seven years old.

to where?
Here.
Grandma retired and built a house.
Next door to where her best friend built a house.

Sweet.
They were like sisters.
Except.
Grandma already had nine sisters.
and three brothers.
At times, grandma would venture off next door.
I would sneak.
Through her things.
In the office.
I always had questions.
Where is my father?
Where is my brother?
Who is my grandfather?
But no one ever answered me.
Dead.
I concluded.
Until.
I went through my grandmother's items in her closet one
summer.
A box.
Filled with pictures
baby announcements
and other papers.
I recognized the name.
Could that be him?
I decided to hold my breath and ask my grandmother when she
came home.
Is that my brother?

Yes, and one day I hope to find him and bring him here, every
summer with you.
Find him?
Why was he missing?
I wrote down all of the information in a notepad.
One day I will find him.

Cousins
We play.
We fight.
We dance.
Dancing was one of our favorite activities.
Spice Girls.
Which one were you?
Everyone assumed I would be Scary Spice.
Curly
wild hair.
I often didn't oppose,
but I would have liked to have a say.
Until this time
I had to wait.
My cousin took out a picture
shoved it in my face and said,
See, you look like your brother!
Like who? I don't have a brother; I have a sister.
Dummy.
No! You do have a brother, go ask my mom.
I, 7 months her senior.
There were many times that I found out family secrets because
of her.
My aunt liked *bonchiche*. That's Spanish for bullshit.
I took the picture and yelled out for my aunt.
Her other daughter was sitting in the corner of the kitchen.

She looked at me.
She had one glass eye.
Wait until your mom gets here and ask her.

I dont know how to begin. I am at a total loss for words. I pray someone has reached you with this regretable news. Your Grandma has passed away, my mother was in a auto accident friday early evening.

I was called to the Chaplin's office about 9:35 pm Saturday nite. ▓▓▓▓▓▓▓▓▓▓ called the jail. ▓▓ and cusin ▓▓▓ where there and I spoke to them all. I am supposed to call Florida tonite. ▓▓▓ said she tried to call you and ▓▓▓. I reminded her you were away. I wont be able to call you until tuesday. The chaplin will be back then to give me a call. You and Grandma are close and I thank the Lord for a least granting me that wish. Me, ▓▓▓▓ I am frazzled, and hurt. I really am holding on or so I

Manslaughter

A hot summer in '99.

Living the teenage dream.

I met a few friends when I moved out of the city.

It was an exciting time in a new environment.

The house phone rang.

Hi grandma! The next moment I later regretted.

I'm sorry grandma, but I won't be visiting Florida this summer.

Pause...

It's just that, since we just moved here, I want to hang out with my new friends.

I might as well have put a knife through her heart myself.

Next, she mentioned making a trip to the mall and asked if I wanted anything.

Selfishly, I replied, *Yes! A cute bathing suit!*

Two weeks later, my family and I returned from a mini road trip.

Ecstatic, I couldn't wait to open my letters and check my answering machine.

I opened up a letter from a friend visiting Colorado.

Cool.

Next, a letter from my dad. A term used here loosely.

Your grandmother has pasted away. My mother was in an auto accident early Friday morning.

Although the spelling of "pasted" was incorrect, it was metaphorically fitting.

I slouched against the wall in the hallway.

Heart pumping.

Blood rushing.

Tears falling.

Bang.

Bang, bang.
Bang, bang, bang, bang, bang, bang...
The back of my head swells.
I continue bashing my head against the wall so I can feel something other than this.
She and a friend were driving to the mall when an 18-wheeler struck her Mazda on I-95.
No bathing suit.

A Hawaiian Sunset.
Photo: Werner Stoy

God
is not too willing.
Why is it always up to his will?
His will granted her trips all over the world
and other places I'm sure I would have asked about if she were
still here.
There were always a lot of questions
but no answers.
Silence.
Stare.
Secrets.
Tears.
Even at her funeral, there was no mention of her only grand-
daughter. Or even a grandson.
Survivors of her death were those who never spoke to me again.
A book of memories lost.
Aunts
great aunts
uncles
great uncles
cousins
and family friends.
Hundreds of people who shared my bloodline.
Ghosted.

Spam
is tasty once it's cooked out of the can.
But to put it raw on your face is a new level.
The house phone rang, and we immediately jumped.
Any day we would receive word of my cousin's death.
Age 32
7-year-old twin girls

2-year-old daughter.
A husband.
Her students.
Her mother.
Her family.
All left behind.
But that call came three weeks after this day.
It took a while to figure out who my mother was talking to
But as soon as I heard mom's voice
I knew I was in deep trouble.

Your grandmother wants to talk to you about her phone bill!
Long distance calls to NY!

I don't want to, and I don't care to talk to her.
I chose the wrong choice of words.

SLAP!

In the kitchen, I could hear laughing.
Fuming and embarrassed, I gingerly walked into the kitchen.
My Spice Girl cousin had a grin on her face.
Haha, she slapped you!
I approached my cousin from behind.
She probably felt the hair standing behind her neck.
Blood boiling inside me.
The words repeating in my head.
Haha, she slapped you!
I lifted my right hand and took one good swing across her face.
She dropped the dishes in the sink and started
screaming,
crying,
wailing on the floor.

I ran out of the kitchen and passed my mom's room.

Mom! She's crying!

My uncle put cold Spam on her face.

Sisters

What if you risked your life
for someone
who later betrayed you?
What if you were able to end your suffering sooner
if you knew
what you did today?
Would you have shouted at the top of your lungs?
Save me! Save me!
Would you ask
if they remembered?
Do you remember when
he told me he would kill you if I said anything?
Do you remember when
he said he would kill mom if I told on him?
Do you remember when
I drove to that girl's house who threatened you?
Do you remember when
you almost got me arrested because you were underage
drinking?
Do you remember when
I used to take you into the city streets at night when they were
fighting?
Do you remember when
I helped you fill out your college applications?
Do you remember when
I gave you my car?

Do you remember when
you totaled it?
Do you remember when
I supported your abortion?
Do you remember when
you physically attacked me when I was pregnant with your
niece?
Do you remember when
we used to make up dances in our room?
Do you remember when we were dancing at a bar and
you started a fight with a local gang in Cali?
Do you remember when attending music festivals
year after year were more important than father's day?
Do you remember when dad died a week before father's day?
Do you remember when we took turns to stay overnight in
hospice
for our great-grandfather?
No.
You couldn't have remembered.
Your stars aren't aligned in the same sky as mine.

Karma

is a funny concept when the odds are in your favor.
There is no such thing as a perfect life
and therefore when something bad happens in one's life
it is instantly connected to a previous sin.
But what if it happens sooner than that?
Fifth grade was one of the best school years I experienced.
A teacher who I looked up to.
Caring.
Fun.
Inspirational.
Nonjudgmental.

One who would not stay in the school in years following.
For a few years, we did not have access to our school
playground
and we had to use the public park.
School trailers.
They were popping up all over the city to accommodate
the rising enrollment.
A few friends and I decided to play basketball.
A present given to me by my uncle.
We started shooting hoops.
Barely reaching the rim.
But it was fun, and we were girls trying to be cool.
A group of young men walked over to us.
High school boys.
Cutting.
Smoking.
Jerks.
This is our court, little girls. Get off.
We were here first.
I opened my mouth. I am an 11-year-old girl.
The high school boy proceeded to take my basketball
and throw it across the yard.
Two of my classmates ran after the ball while
one of the boys jumped to reach the rim.
He caught it.
Hung on to it with one hand.
The rest of his group of delinquents
laughing.
Cheering.
Showing off.
But then
DROP.
He fell off the rim and landed under his arm.

He wailed.

We laughed.

Hard.

His boy walked over to us.

Do you think that's funny?

Giggling.

Yes........

The rest of the group helped his friend get up from the floor.

He was holding on to his dangling arm.

His friend was visibly pissed off.

At this point, I started to get nervous.

The boy got in our face and started cursing us out.

I heard the school whistle blow but did not move.

Students all lined up with their classes

Teachers escorting them inside the building

Me, frozen

The boys lifted their friend off the ground and started to walk toward the street

What happens next?

I wish I could remember details.

How did a gun end up against my temple?

My principal yells out to the boys

Incoherent to me

They yell back, motioning to each other to jump in the white car

I noticed my friends crying

Why am I not crying?

I don't say a word

Calculate every move

The world stood still

Once the boys got in the car

The one who tempted my brain with a pistol

Quit the screaming match with my principal

He threw me to the ground and jumped in the back seat
Later
At the police station
The officers asked for specific descriptions about the boys and
took my statement
All the while I wondered if my backpack was still leaning
against the fence in the yard,
I had homework to do.

Ex boyfriend

I am sorry for making you grow up faster than you needed to.
I am sorry for the pain and anguish I suffered and that you
endured.
I am sorry you had to be strip-searched before you came to
visit me.
I am sorry the hospital wouldn't let me call you.
I am sorry I cut myself with a blade.
I am sorry I tried to end my life.
I am sorry you had to meet my spirits.
I am sorry you had to remind me to take my medication.
But most of all
I am sorry you had to hold my deepest darkest secrets to your-
self and never tell a soul.

Hey sweetie, what's going on? Nuttin huh? Same here. A boring ass day. Listen, I dunno what to do anymore. It seems my being there makes you worse, and now all we do is fight and you say my NOT being there is worse and you think I don't care or wanna bother with you anymore. I honestly don't know what to say. You keep threatening us with acts of violence against yourself, and you can't do that. That's like external hostage taking, like what David held against you. And you will undoubtedly read these words and think to yourself, "he doesn't care." But I DO care, I really do. I just can't handle this as well as I had hoped. It's becoming a constant thing. It seems as though I can't say or do anything without invoking the wrath of God upon me. I'd love to just be able to hold you in my arms, or lie there and just pretend nothing was wrong, but I can't because we both KNOW something is wrong. And I feel helpless to change it. What do we do now? How long can you pretend nothing's wrong? How long can I cope with it? I just don't know. I dunno how you feel about me anymore. It seems like I just hurt you, and that hurts me more than you can imagine. I wish I could fix everything, I'd give anything to fix it, but I can't, at least not alone. I need you to tell me what you want me to do. Don't tell me to do whatever I want, because you KNOW what I want. I want you to tell me what to do to help, and then you have to let me help. I'll do whatever it takes, because I love you, and you mean the world to me. I leave the choices open to you, I'll support you anyway you go.

Love Always,

P.S.
Don't read this as anger, or frustration, because it's not. It's desperation to make things between us like they were, and not with all the fighting and troubles. I hope you want the same thing.

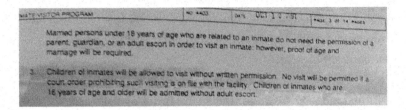

MATE VISITOR PROGRAM   NO. #403   DATE   OCT 1 0 '91   PAGE 3 of 14 PAGES

Married persons under 18 years of age who are related to an inmate do not need the permission of a parent, guardian, or an adult escort in order to visit an inmate; however, proof of age and marriage will be required.

3.   Children of inmates will be allowed to visit without written permission. No visit will be permitted if a court order prohibiting such visiting is on file with the facility. Children of inmates who are 16 years of age and older will be admitted without adult escort.

Inmates

Children of inmates will be allowed to visit without written permission. No visit will be permitted if a court order prohibiting such visiting is on file with the facility. Children of inmates who are 16 years of age and older will be admitted without adult escort.

Normal teenagers wait for their 16th birthday for a driver's permit.

Some have a sweet 16.

Some wait for their first kiss.

Others get their first job.

And then there are a few like me.

Who prepare for their first visit to a correctional facility.

Visitors

The letter has arrived with the instructions.

Approved.

Soon I will be able to visit my biological father in prison.

This would be the first time seeing him in person

At least knowing it's him

We have crossed paths in the past

But I thought he was just a friend of my grandmother

At least that's what she told me

I believed her

Somewhat

It wasn't soon afterward that I got my license that I insisted on taking the drive to visit

He had moved prisons to be closer to me

He said

It was like a girl's first date

I could not arrive looking busted

My mother raised me
And he needed to see that
The day arrived, and I was nervous driving to the correctional
facility
Would the guards let me in?
I am only 16.
I can feel my armpits getting wet
Heart racing
Dry mouth
What will he think of me?
Did I do my hair right?
Did I wear the right clothes?
Would he be proud?
I would never know.
I arrived.
He didn't show up.

June 17, 20__

Dear Princess,

What's going on my love? Tell ████ Hello for me.

I am writing ████ to ask you to please come up here this weekend coming Sat/Sun 8:30am to 2:00pm, I want you to come by at least 12, ~~come at anytime ___ ___ ___~~ Muhammad must come to the mountain. I wrote your Mother, but I decided against mailing it, (BECAUSE I told you I would NOT tell HER) But you and I need to speak, No! I am not mad, but I will tell you how to get out of this mess without getting in trouble. Please take this letter seriously, Plus Princess Sky, I have some new jokes I hope you chuckle at! i.o.l

I understand why you did not come today the storm watch, I miss you but I'd rather you not drive in that type of weather. So I really expect to see you ~~next~~ week, meaning this weekend.

Your Mother did a good job raising you, I am really proud of my Sky all around, there is just somethings you need to know and your Father is the one who going to tell you. You have done nothing wrong, so its not some lecture type of visit o.k. Your Father is for real when it comes to something like this. I would ask if you have the money on hand, I ask that you bring Dad

22

about (ten bags of large chips)
(5 packs of cookies)
(12 bananas)
(A few bags of candies)

If you can bring this I will give you the money spent, plus. I ask because I am really nervous about the board and I am eating like a large pig.

But all in all, I will see you on the weekend. I wrote Aunt Cathy and told her I will take care of this as a family. So, much love to myself. No excuse for not coming, even if you can't afford the items its o.k. I still want to see you. Tell Mona Hello! and it was nice talking to her, And you my love don't worry everything will be fine.

Love Always
Dad ♥

1 Taken
too soon.
Never again to be
hugged
kissed
loved
or to share stories.
days ago, when writing this,
a friend died in a tragic accident.
His wife...pregnant.
a toddler for a daughter
left behind.

2 Taken
too soon.
Murder.
She was in high school.
Living the dream.
A boyfriend who we thought was 19.
Really he was in his mid-20s.
Undocumented Immigrant.
Took the sweet life of my friend's sister.
Strangled.
Life in prison.

3 Taken
too soon.
suicide.
Bullet to her head.
Boyfriend didn't want to keep the baby.
She couldn't take it anymore.
22 years young.

A friendship lost forever.

Death

is inevitable.
No one asked us to be born
yet most of the time,
we are not in control of when
we die.
Death is the final resting spot.
The one living will know all too well one day.
What is life really anyway?

Going through a moody mode
Taking only the easy road
Going through all of life's surprises
Wearing all of life's disguises
Knowing only your own true self
Crying for a need of help
Knowing that you will only do
The only thing life wants you to
So what is it you are going through?
Life...it's the only thing you have to do.

Suicide

I grabbed the steering wheel from the passenger seat.
I could hear my mom yelling but I did not care.
My 8-year-old sister was in the back seat.
Not sure what was happening.
Probably frightened.
I was emotionless.
We were driving home from the police station.
Shoplifting.
Me and another friend. Her idea.

But I went along with it.
She stole jewelry.
They caught it on camera.
We were arrested.
We were teenagers.
My mom was called.
I sat in the holding cell not knowing what was going to happen.
At that moment, I told myself that I did not care.
Once my mom came to pick me up, I knew there was going to
be harsh
consequences.
That's when I couldn't take the lecture anymore.
I couldn't take this life.
I could not handle being who I am
so it's better off if there was none of me left to worry.
She grabbed the steering wheel back and the car
swerved in and out of the lane.
I failed.
I couldn't even commit suicide.
I tried to end all of our lives.
I failed again.

No Promises

There are times where you make promises to yourself.
Thoughts in your head ping-pong back and forth.
It will happen.
I will tell someone *again*.
I cannot allow myself to start a new life at 14 just to realize
it really did not restart.
It is the same.
Only a different person.
How can there be two?
Who will believe me now?

My biggest mistake was not admitting to
it simultaneously.
It could have been one bird with two stones.
But how many stones should you have if it's
two birds?

10/11/99

Hey sweetie, what's up? How are you? Better I hope. I miss you so much. But don't hurry back. I want you to be as good as you can be. I don't wanna see you sad anymore. It's not fair, it's not your fault. Are you doing ok there? I'm gonna come back and visit you as soon as I can, as often as I can. You don't understand how great it felt to see you again. You had me so worried. Your mom must know me like a book by now. We spent a lot of time together. I think your family likes me. (Hope so!) Your mom didn't know who ███ was, he came up in a conversation. I told her and she laughed. That was pretty cool. Is Pikachu keeping you company? I hope so. Life here is the same. I have way too much work. I haven't been able to concentrate lately. I guess you know why. Funny things happened though. Rocco got shot in the balls during a paintball game and cried (or so I'm told). Cool huh? Coolage. Smile for me, ok? Chemistry sucks, the homework was soooo boring. I'll keep notes and stuff for ya. Your mom really cares about you, you know that right? She was crying on the way home, she really wants you to be happy. We all love you so much ███████ is the medication making you feel bad? What is it like there? Oh yeah, guess what! Come on, guess! Give up? I love you! See, you always win that game! Don't worry about me, or anyone else right now. Concentrate on getting well again. Nothing else matters. NOTHING. I can't even think about you being unhappy anymore. No one should have to go through what you have.

Cool, my kitten just tried to eat my shoes. Now I have to punish him! Ha, a water gun! Hehehe, now he's wet ██████, do you mean it when you say you love me? Because I know for certain, more so than I ever have in my life, that I mean it when I say it to you. Please, just try to feel better. Do what it takes to get better. I'll be here for you no matter what. Nothing will change that. AHHH! My cat bit my toe! Hahaha! Take that, now I have your tail, AHH! No biting! I'll mess up your fur, HAHAHAHA! oops, OW! Little punk. Oh well. But hey, guess what? I dunno, it's your turn to ask! If I don't get to see you soon, try to write me a note or something, have your mom give it to me! But, it's 1:00 a.m. now so I guess I should go. Sweet dreams. May all your wishes come true.

I love you.

Love Always,

███████

Diary entry: 4/3/2000
"I have a confession to make. I am not proud of myself.
I don't want to talk about it in therapy because they will send me back
to the psychiatric hospital.
I sliced my wrist, burned it with a lighter. Then I sliced my leg and burned it
with a match. I was so stressed out, so I gave up.
I am such a loser. I wish I didn't hurt myself.
But what's done is done."

Waiting
Summer after high school.
I made it.
College around the corner.
New doors.
New opportunities.
A new life.
I waited at my boyfriend's parents' house for the phone call.
He should be out any minute now.
My car is full of gas and ready for the trip.
I don't mind driving.
Even if it is late at night.
The waiting is what's killing me.
Should I go out to dinner?
No. I must be in a quiet place so I can hear my cell phone ring.
My boyfriend looks over to me from time to time.
He looks at me checking my phone.
His mom makes me dinner.
We watch the news.
Something we started doing daily after 9/11.
My phone buzzes.

Is it the jail?
Not him.
I put my phone back down and look up.
Nope. It's not him.
We eat dinner and no one dares to ask me any questions.
The night continues on.
I decide to head back home.
I do not want anyone to see my face when I cry.
He never called.

April 3rd 2002

Dear Princess,

What's up sweetheart? I have a question for you; I am wondering if you might want to come to pick me up when I get released if possible?

I was just thinking and I figured I'd write. I don't know the date but I go in June 01 and if yes about 45 days after that, even tough this is the last one. they can still hold me for 1 year after that and I would miss your graduation by 2 months, but the bright side I get to be with you, I ask God for his strength so I can be the Father I've always wanted to be. But changing to other things, ████████████? and everyone!? And ████ me, how is she holding up? Hey Princess, your Father is at a lost for words, Please help me find the, o.k.

I will tell you about a story I wrote in the Journal already, a true one.

I was on my way to your house, where you and Laurie stayed, I was coming from Queens, Well when I got there you, was like Daddy—come here, do that, let me show you, How come? You remembered me. Well I beleived you were 3 or 4 years old. You and I were playing and by accident, you poked me on the eye, I jumped up and cussed, you jetted to the corner but I was not upset with you, I didn't know it yet that the cornea (The White) was scratched and everytime I blinked, Wow! But looking back

I LOVE YOU
PRINCESS
SKY♥
DAD

31

College

I couldn't afford it.

I couldn't dorm.

I couldn't endure the extra costs of living.

I was always a good student.

One who looked at school as a gateway out of hell.

If I succeed, I can be who I want to be.

It was difficult for me to get a loan.

Mom did not want to sign off on one.

I had no credit.

Eventually, she gave in.

But only for one year.

The rest I had to figure out on my own.

I cried. Many nights.

How was it fair that I got accepted to college and cannot afford it?

It was a new reality I did not want to face.

But I did.

I attended.

I lied on my loan application year after year.

I accepted the lifetime debt.

I needed to prove I was more than just a statistic.

Two psychiatric stays during my high school tenure.

Racial profiling by suburban principals.

Dodging slurs from classmates.

Inappropriate comments from teachers.

A city education competing with a suburban education.

Hormones.

Teenage life.

In the end,

I chose the right college.

People who were just like me.

Straight up.
Real.
Forgiving.

Drug House

I want you to have the bedroom set.

What am I going to do with a bedroom set?
At 15 years old, I did not have the authority to make that
decision.
I live in a condo.
My mother's condo.
The furniture is also over a thousand miles away.
I decline.
Sorry. I cannot take grandma's set.
She wrote a check for me for $2,500.
I gave it to my mother.
She deposited it into her bank account.
She said I owed her for fixing my car.
The one I use for college.
The college I couldn't afford.
Grandma's house was sold.
Items in the house were sold.
The money was saved for my father when he got out of jail.
The same money he used to buy drugs.

▮▮▮ I am selling the house for a good profit. I could never sleep in there, I respect grandma and all but certain things I wont do. I am using the money to get a place in your county or ▮▮▮▮▮▮▮▮▮. Is that o.k with you sky? Sleep well love.

I Love you
Beautiful

Advice
Four months after no communication
the house phone rings.
Mom picks up.
Who's this? Oh.

The way she was talking, I knew it was someone she did not
want to talk to.
In the last few years of communicating through letters
Mom did not want anything to do with him.
She respected my decision to build a relationship with him.
This time
She wasn't having it.
She asked him where he had been all these months.
Back in jail.
A violation of his parole the day he got out.
I looked into her room and gestured that I was on my way out.
This time it was for good.

...there's something I wanted to tell you. People in this world are funny & cold why because they do things that are very hurtful to other people. The key is to dont let what someone do effect your outlook on life. People may do things just to get a reaction from you. Dont allow a twisted mind to twist yours. Keep hope, God and love on the forefront while remembering the evil and Malice that people are capable of. Men as well as Woman. You hold a future for you. You decide what that future will be. I'm the always for you I love you dearly from your little boy too to the tip of your head. I'm just telling you to embrace the goodness in god, and you will see love for yourself.

Dad

Too Late

I often wondered if it was a mistake.

To tell him the truth.

Did he cry?

Did he feel powerless in his cell?

Did he talk about it with other cellmates?

It wasn't part of the agenda to make him feel at fault.

Evidently, there was nothing he could have done to prevent it.

Guilt.

It was the guilt of being absent.

It was the guilt of being denied the ability to seek revenge.

It was the guilt of not being the father he could have been.

What would he have done?

Would he have chased him #1 out of the apartment like my
uncle?

Would he have removed him #2 from his house like my cousin?

Either way, it was too late.

Too late for all the men in my life.

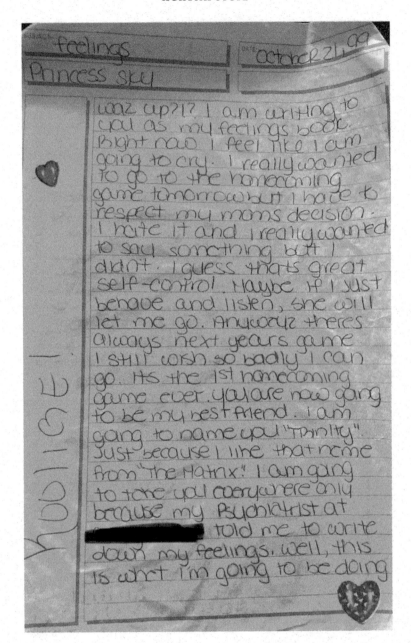

feelings | DATE October 21, 99

Princess Sky

Waz up?!? I am writing to you as my feelings book. Right now I feel like I am going to cry. I really wanted to go to the homecoming game tomorrow but I have to respect my moms decision. I hate it and I really wanted to say something but I didnt. I guess thats great self-control. Maybe if I just behave and listen, she will let me go. Anywayz theres always next years game. I still wish so badly I can go. Its the 1st homecoming game ever. You are now going to be my best friend. I am going to name you "Trinity". Just because I like that name from "The Matrix." I am going to take you everywhere only because my psychiatrist at ▓▓▓▓▓▓ told me to write down my feelings. well, this is what I'm going to be doing

38

okay, I am still writing tou It is 9:26pm and it feels good to be home. This is so weird. My mom might let me go tomorrow if me and ███ take ███████ I think it is a good deal. I really feel weird though going tomorrow knowing that people are going to be asking me alot of questions. 2B home it feels retarded b/c I feel slow. Only b/c of the medication. I'm used to talking fast + thinking quicker. It takes a while to speak 4me anyway. I am going to see how my last dosage makes me feel. (It is going to take a long time to adjust!) I Just felt mad. It is 10:05 + my mom just told me to shut off my phone + beeper. I am suppose to be expecting 3 phone calls only I that is important (1) ███████ ████ and ██████ can wait. I hope I can continue to write my feelings down and don't spaz out oh god please!

Self-Control
The urge to say or do something.
The "needs improvement" on your report card.
The back hand to your mouth.
Blood dripping from your busted lip.
The uncontrollable tics.
The undiagnosed ADHD.
I was always bored.
Unchallenged.
Misunderstood.
Sit still.
Stop jumping.
No roughhousing.
Shut up.
Write down your feelings.
No one wants to hear them.

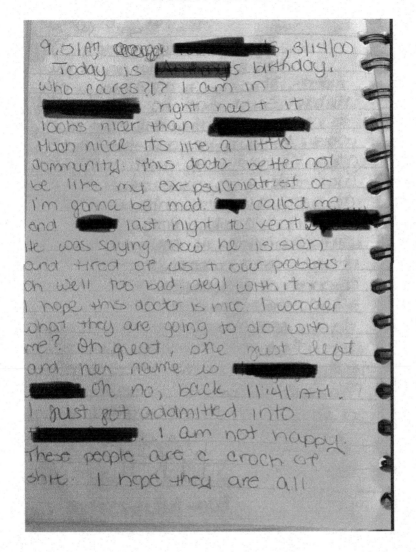

9:01 AM, ████████ ████████, 3/14/00
Today is ████████'s birthday.
Who cares?!? I am in
████████ right now + it
looks nicer than ████████
Much nicer. Its like a little
community. This doctor better not
be like my ex-psychiatrist or
I'm gonna be mad. ██ called me
and ██ last night to vent. ████████
He was saying how he is sick
and tired of us + our problems.
Oh well too bad. deal with it.
I hope this doctor is nice. I wonder
what they are going to do with
me? Oh great, she just left
and her name is ████████
████ Oh no, back 11:41 AM.
I just got addmitted into
████████, I am not happy.
These people are c croch of
shit. I hope they are all

going to die. I want to
go home. I know what
I saw + I am keeping
it that way. As long as I
can keep writing in here this
will be my one and true friend.
Now I am going to be here
for a long time. whatever!!
This is such a croch of
shit. I can't believe this.
This is going to mess me up
badly. I told my teacher that
if I had to stay then I will
escape. I'm wondering about
that now. I won't do it though
because that will be stupid of
me. I should've not made up a
story and said that I was lying
and All I needed was attention.
But I know that that would be
a lie. I hate this. I never
thought that I would enter a
psychiatric center (again) for that

matter. Things are going to be so different when I get out of here. Now my uncle wants to ask me a question. Maybe I should just use my power to shut him up. That could be funny. Now he's saying that I have an attitude. I told my mom that I am mad at her + not to come visit me or pick me up. I hate my fucking life. I wish I just fucking die now. I hate my fucking life. can't these people just leave me alone. Shut the fuck up ███. Oh god. I am going to get the hell out of here. I hate this place. Actually, I'm going to stay here. I might like it here. I might even live here. My uncle is getting me mad. so is my

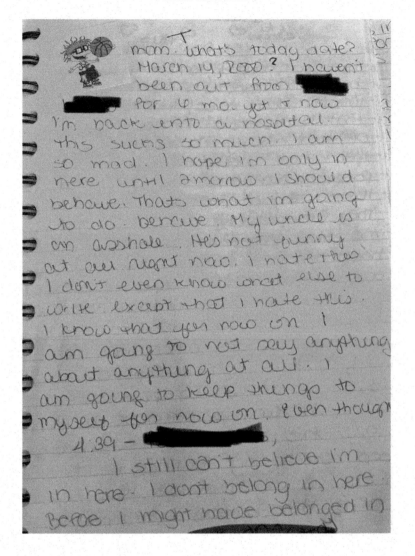

mom. what's today date? March 14, 2000? I haven't been out from ▓▓▓ for 6 mo. yet I now I'm back into a hospital this sucks to much. I am so mad. I hope I'm only in here until tomorrow. I should behave. Thats what I'm going to do. behave. My uncle is an asshole. He's not funny at all right now. I hate this. I don't even know what else to write except that I hate this. I know that fer now on I am going to not say anything about anything at all. I am going to keep things to myself fer now on. Even though

4.39 - ▓▓▓▓▓▓▓,

I still can't believe I'm in here. I dont belong in here. Before I might have belonged in

here but now I don't. All
do of hallucinations and illusions
which I don't have, I believe
that I saw true things, instead
of them having me don't have
then they should have me
personally evaluated. I don't need
to be around these people.
They are probably going to have
me stay longer since they
have to also keep an eye on
everyone else. Most people here
seem nice, otherwise I don't need
to be here. It's kind of on
to stay here but otherwise no
way, man. I am going to
progress as much as possible.
Not cause any problems or anything.
I love this book. I just wanna
keep writing my feelings in it
as long as no one finds it.
I hope ████ comes with my

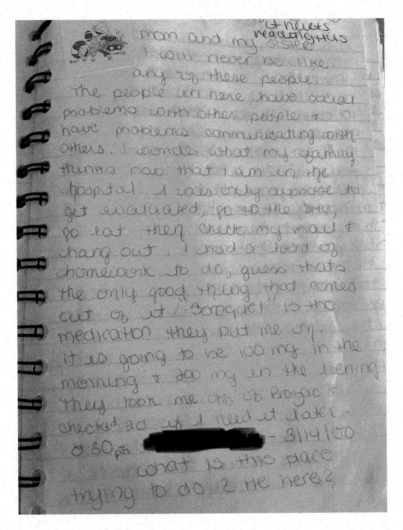

mom and my sister *thiets reading this*
I will never be like
any of these people.
The people in here have social
problems with other people &
have problems communicating with
others. I wonder what my family
thinks now that I am in the
hospital. I was only suppose to
get evaluated, go to the DMV,
go eat then check my mail &
hang out. I had a load of
homework to do, guess thats
the only good thing that comes
out of it. "Seroquel" is the
medication they put me on.
It is going to be 100 mg in the
morning & 200 mg in the evening.
They took me off of Prozac &
checked to if I used it later.
0:30 pm ▬▬▬▬▬▬ - 3/14/00
what is this place
trying to do 2 me here?

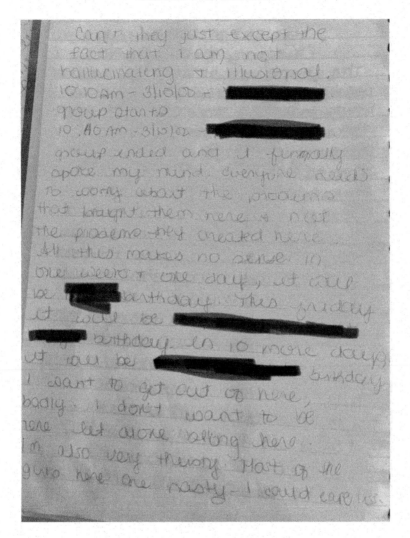

Can't they just except the fact that I am not hallucinating + illusional.
10:10am - 3/10/00 - ████████
group starts
10:40am - 3/10/00 - ████████
group ended and I finally spoke my mind. everyone needs to worry about the problems that brought them here + not the problems they created here. All this makes no sense. In one week + one day, it will be ████████ birthday. This friday it will be ██████████████ birthday. In 10 more days it will be ██████████████ birkday. I want to get out of here, badly. I don't want to be here let alone getting here. I'm also very theory that of the guts here are nasty - I could care les.

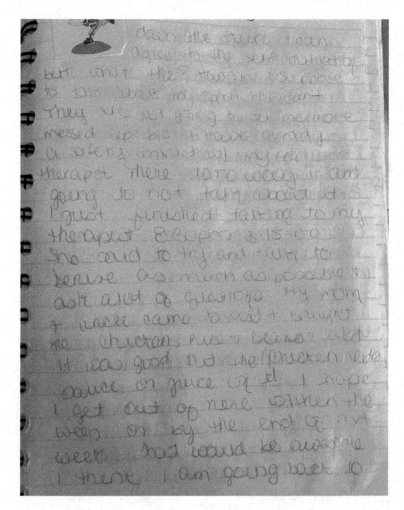

Save Me

Hiking
through the woods on a warm spring day
El Nino weather they called it
Walking on this beaten path
Where did this happen? Show me!
Why did she make me bring her back here?
She is lost.
She wants to understand me
Understand what broke me
Understand who was reaching out to me
I showed her where it all went down
I pointed in the direction of where I heard her voice.
Save me. She said.
The girl dashed from tree to tree until...
I woke up with my boyfriend standing over me
Calling my name over and over and over again
Wake up! Please wake up!
Is this the story my mom wants me to relive?
I showed her the map that I sketched.
She promised me that I would only speak to the psychiatrist to
let them know what happened.
Was it a seizure?
Did I hallucinate someone being there?
Next came tests.
EKG
EEG
No indication of a seizure.
Softball team cut me.
Too risky.
First season playing. Gone.
Second time in a psychiatric hospital.

Who is going to save me?

Diagnosis
Schizophrenic
Post-traumatic stress disorder
Manic depressive
Suicidal
How will I define myself now?
Seroquel
Prozac
Risperdal
How will it make me feel now?
New words added to my vocabulary bank.
Exposure.
More of my childhood dwindling.
Do other teens my age know these words?
Are they stamped with this stigma like me?
Will I ever recover?

Secrets
This wasn't just a secret.
It was a survival tool.
If I spilled the beans
People would die.
Myself included.
The detective sits across from me.
A family friend.
A favor.
Tell me everything you feel comfortable with saying
I say nothing.
I have always said nothing.
My brain is the one who keeps chatting.
My mouth is silent.

The detective looked at me.
Let's start with what happened the day you ran out of the apartment. Why did you run?
I thought hard about his question.
He gave me time to think about it.
I shifted in my seat.
Without looking at him, I began...
It started with a phone call from my grandmother...

Grandma

I should have treated her better.
I took advantage of her always being there for me.
After losing both maternal grandparents before the age of 8
She played a pivotal role in my childhood.
Taking the absence of her son.
What did I want from her?
Everything.
As if she were to take the place of her son
and succumb to my demands.
Disney World?
Check.
Beach trip?
Check.
Clothes?
Check.
Money?
Check.
Movies?
Check.
Magazines from the supermarket?
Check.
Portable TV?
Not so fast.

There were some things she did not let me have.
For instance.
The truth.
Who is my grandfather?
Silence.
Is he alive?
Silence.
Where did you get married?
Silence.
What is his name?
Silence
Does he know about me or my half-brother?
Silence. A tear drops from her face.
I guess I was not the only one keeping secrets.

Facebook
first came out when I was in college.
College students with an .edu email only.
Until it opened up to the rest of the world.
This may be the moment I've been waiting for.
I often searched for his name.
Looking to find my half-brother.
I had his birth date.
Announcement card.
My mom knew his mother's name.
A discussion we had in the hospital waiting room.
While waiting the final breaths of my aunt.
The one who used to babysit him.
It has been over 20 years since he has been born.
Does he know about me?
Two months later
I found out.
He knows who I am.

A message was in my Facebook inbox.
But I did not recognize the name.
Who is this contacting me?

Transcript

Facebook User 1: (3/15/2009 12:58:31 PM): I am here

Facebook User ME: (3/15/2009 1:01:07 PM): i was saying before i lost connection that i didnt hear from *him* until i was 14 years old when i was at my grandomthers house and he called collect on the phone, before that i did not know where he was the entire time since i was 4.

Facebook User 1: (3/15/2009 1:01:38 PM): wow. I thought for sure he would stay in contact with you

Facebook User ME: (3/15/l2009 1:01:42 PM): no one told me that he was in jail the entire time.

Facebook User 1: (3/15/2009 1:01:54 PM): I did not know either

Facebook User ME: (3/15/2009 1:02:33 PM): nope, he wrote me a letter at my grandmothers and then we wrote back and forth for about three years and when i was 17, he was suppose to come out of jail... i was going to pick him up on that day since we sort of developed a relationship via mail but on the day he came out he never called me

Facebook User 1: (3/15/2009 1:03:55 PM): wow. I stopped hearing from him when *his son* was one...and your aunt was babysitting him

Facebook User ME: (3/15/2009 1:04:40 PM): he called my moms house like three months later and she cursed him out and said never to call again. he tried to write but we moved and went further north so if he tried to write, the mail did not forward to me...

Facebook User 1: (3/15/2009 1:16:45 PM): but i don't remember what year

Facebook User ME: (3/15/2009 1:18:40 PM): yeah he has been jumping around from prison to prison and from the last i heard, he was out and getting married this year. I heard only bc one of my moms old friends said he ran into some old friends. So its interesting bc its still a small world but i dont care to contact him. he had his first chance as his rights as a father and the second one he def. blew with me so he would never be a part of my life... well the last letter i got form him said that a doctor told him he did not have time left to live and blah blah blah but i didnt believe him and didnt respond, but it was the last letter b4 we moved again... so if you dont mind me asking, what ahppened with Michael?

Facebook User 1: (3/15/2009 1:35:22 PM): well he was always such a wonderful kid i never thought i would have to worry about him getting into trouble... but because i was working 12 hour shifts sometimes 7 days a week, michael started hanging out with a bad crowd and started doing drugs... i had lost my job in the factory and was working as a waitress in december of 2005 i got a phone call from the police that michael was arrested for trying to pass counterfit money... i was already fed up with his drug use and stealing from me by this point, i told the police i did not want to pick him up from jail because i wanted to teach him a lesson... I just wanted him to get help... mike went to juvinille detention and was doing so well there... but then at his trial the judge told me this is not a rich county and if i want him to stay in jail i have to pay for him to stay there... they took him and put him in foster care saying that i wanted to get rid of him... but that was not true... i knew if he did not get help from somewhere he would end up like his father and this was my worst nightmare... he got thrown out of the foster care program because of underage drinking but still would not come back to live with me...he is in jail in indiana now and gets released on april 13

Facebook User ME: (3/15/2009 2:13:52 PM): i dont know what happened in the past but i do know that somewhere down the line, my grandmother wished she knew michael. the only thing i can think of is that she realized her son wasn't who she thought he was and came to realization about that...her sisters took all of her belongings and out them in storage and when *he* got out if jail, they saw him and gave it ALL to him and he sold it for drugs

Facebook User 1: (3/15/2009 2:23:04 PM): did you visit her in florida much

Facebook User ME: (3/15/2009 2:23:42 PM): i went almost every summer and the one summer i didnt go is when she died...

St. Patrick's Day
Riding the metro train
Downtown
Not expecting anything
But butterflies.
This was the day.

We went to a bar because it was open early for cops.
Green beers
Shots
Leprechauns
Bagpipes.
It was only a matter of hours before I would meet him.
Would I recognize him?
We have never met.
I looked at the clock on the wall of the bar.
It was almost time.
I told my friends that I would meet them later.
I walked over to the public park where we decided on meeting.
I am still a young girl in my 20s.
Public
Daylight
And my cop friends close-by.
As I approached the eastern side of the park
the scene was uncanny.
Was I looking at a mirror image?
He looked just like me.
It had been almost a year since he got out of jail.
We mostly kept in touch through writing emails.
He messed up his life.
He wanted to get back on track.
He wanted to meet his half-sister.
My stomach was queasy, and I knew it wasn't from the alcohol.
I walked up to him and spoke
Wow, we really do look alike.
The streets buzzed around us, filled with people celebrating the
holiday.
We were both dressed in green.
Appropriate.
It was the first and the last day we met in person.

There isn't much to say when the last few years of your
adulthood
has been better than his.
I didn't want him to think that although we shared the same
absent father
my life still seemed better than his.

Milk

Humans should not drink another mammal's milk.
I stopped immediately after kindergarten.
A white substance that spoils in the heat.
Sticky
Unforgiving smell
Gag.
When did the first incident occur?
The male cop stared at me, and I took a deep breath in.
I was about eight.
He looked at me and scribbled on his legal pad.
How can you remember that you were eight years old?
His eyes squinted.
Is this an interrogation or an investigation?
I remember because we just moved to a new apartment.
He writes some more.
I was always blessed with remembering dates because I
connected them with major life events.
Did he want me to continue?
My stomach was already in knots.
At this point
All I wanted to do was go home.
The noise of the outside city streets was loud and buzzing.
Inside the precinct, there was minor chatter among police
officers.
He looks up at me again.

What is he going to ask me next?
I look over my shoulder to my mother.
Since I am only 14 years old, she has a right to accompany me.
A part of me hoped she walked away so she didn't have to bear the pain.
This would become a theme between us.
I remained silent.
The officer looked down at his legal pad and scribbled some more.
I drift deep into my thoughts and prayed the flashbacks will go away.
But just like milk
They continue to spoil my mind.

Popeye

Since we moved around a lot
I have always remembered when things happened.
It was easy to narrow down the date when I had a starting point.
My entire year in kindergarten and half of first grade
Was spent living in an apartment building that had no elevator.
At first, it was just me and my mom.
Until
She brought *him* home.
I had my own bedroom with all my belongings.
Mom slept on the pull-out couch.
She would read me bedtime stories such as
The Three Billy Goats Gruff, repeatedly.
Even as a kid
I admired the way the last goat stood up for himself and his brothers.
Something I neglected to do for myself.
This *guy* brought over a VCR to our apartment.

We were able to watch movies and soon started to collect our
own VHS tapes.
One tape in my possession was the cartoon flick
Popeye.
He was my hero and I enjoyed watching him save Olive Oyl.
One early morning I was the first to wake.
Mom and *guy* were sleeping in the living room on the
sofa bed.
I quietly snuck into the room and turned on the tv.
I wanted to watch my hero.
I took out the VHS tape and slipped it into the VCR.
But nothing came on the TV.
I pressed all of the buttons on the VCR, but nothing seemed to
work.
He woke up and saw me on the floor
Messing with the VCR.
Busted.
Not just me
but the VCR.
He begins to scream.
I flinched and immediately started crying.
His screams alerted my mother to wake.
She turned over to me now.
Yelling.
I ran to my room and hid under the covers.
I can hear him screaming that I put the VHS tape backward
into the VCR.
It was going to cost a lot of money to retrieve the tape.
My mother enters my room and reprimands me on touching
someone else's
Property without permission.
I hated him.
I hated the look in his eyes when he yelled at me.

I just didn't know then how much I would hate him in the future.

Turbulence

It wasn't long before we moved out of the walk-up apartment.
Our next place was on the other side of the city.
This would be my second elementary school.
A baby was on the way.
This apartment had three bedrooms.
The living room was huge
And we had a dining room this time.
I was happy about the new place.
The school, however,
Not so much.
Entering in the middle of a first-grade year was hard.
I had no friends.
I was new to the neighborhood.
We had family gatherings often.
Especially after my sister was born.
Soon the apartment became associated as a turbulent period.
My grandfather died.
He was an alcoholic.
My uncle got stabbed on the subway.
He was on drugs.
The family was trying to hold it together.
I didn't know at the time,
But I was trying to hold it together myself.

Punished

I was punished
A lot.
There was a fire inside of me
That I never understood.

School was boring.
So I talked.
A lot.
I would finish my work ahead of others.
Bored.
At home,
I felt as if no one would listen to me.
A new baby around was challenging.
She was my sister.
She was really cute.
She looked nothing like me.
Kids after school would approach my babysitter when she
Picked me up and asked who that baby was.
She is my sister.
They would laugh and say there is no way she is my sister.
Her skin is white.
Her hair is blonde.
Mine were neither.
I wondered why we looked so different
But I knew she was my sister.
A lot started to change back at home.
He was meaner.
He looked at me as a
Nuisance
Annoying
Brat.
I could feel his despisement toward me.
My mouth responded back.
Mom would punish me.
My room was my safe haven.
I could feel as if I escaped
Being on the other side of the apartment.
One day I got it bad.

No punishment.
Just blows.
I was used to a backhand in the mouth
Here and there.
But this time
I was on the floor.
Kicked in the stomach.
Kicked on my side when I turned over.
What did I do this time?
That's the tricky thing about memories.
Some flashbacks don't offer explanations.
Just vivid images.

Rocking Chair
Before third grade started
We moved again.
This time it was into a two-bedroom apartment.
Rent controlled.
Third new elementary school.
It wasn't as easy to hide in a smaller apartment.
I had to share my room with my sister.
She was only a year old at the time.
Slept mostly in my mother's room with *him*.
There was a TV in their room, and at times
I would lay with her to help her go to sleep.
What is the rocking chair?
I ponder on this question the officer asked me.
He would lay behind me in bed.
Push me against him and rock.
I remember laying there and not wanting to wake my sister.
What is an 8-year-old to do?
I thought at first it was a game to get her to sleep.
But she was already sleeping.

I felt his penis on my buttocks get hard.
He would rock slow.
Then harder.
This would happen a few times.
Until
One time he reached his hand over to mine.
Moved it behind me so I can feel how hard he was.
Then
Milk.

Eleven

Teachers leave an impression on young students
Fifth-grade year was one of them
She was
Sweet
Kind
Nonjudgmental.
When she yelled at the other students,
You vicariously felt her pain.
She never yelled.
She was the only teacher I could confide in
About my secret.
There were many times
I would stay during lunch and help her set up the classroom.
I would share stories of the parental struggles in my household.
Nothing about *him* and me.
Not yet.
I took my time on every project she assigned.
I wanted to impress her.
Show her I was more than just her student.
A part of me wished she was my mom.
I could be her daughter.
I knew she would never hurt me.

I told her about a fight that broke out at home.
Spilled the details of the fight between my mom and *him*.
He left.
He said he was never coming back.
I was full of glee.
This year started a clear and positive outlook for my family.
My uncle was going to get the treatment he needed.
He was being released from the drug rehab hospital
and was setting up his new life across the country.
Mom said we would visit him for Christmas.
It would only be the three of us. Forever.
Months after we returned from our trip across the country,
My sister experienced a devastating fall.
She needed surgery.
It happened on *his* watch.
Visitation rights.
Weekends.
She was months shy of four.
Mom would sue the establishment.
They would settle for funding her college
When she turned 18.
The separation was a pivotal change
In my life.
Until the end of fifth grade
He returned.
Begging for forgiveness.
Apologized for the fights
And arguments.
He will be better.
Soon afterward
I knew someone needed to know
What he had done to me.
What he was going to continue doing to me.

I was almost free.
That was the year I received *that* gift
From my uncle.
A basketball.
The one I brought to school.
Recess.
Gun to the head.
I often thought about the trigger being pulled.
The event paralleled my life.
Uncertainty.
Victimized.
No justice.
My teacher comforted us in the classroom after it happened.
She is the one.
The one I will tell.
The one I will share my secrets with.
I just needed time.
Time to gather my thoughts.
Time to tell her that if she told authorities about *him*
It would risk the lives of my mother and sister.
The lives *he* often threatened me with
If you ever tell anyone what I did to you, they will die.
Do you want that to happen?
No.
I let it happen.
I allowed him to touch me.
I allowed him to put his hands in my underwear.
Someone needed to know.
Summer vacation was quickly approaching.
I will muster up the courage to
Find her classroom
Tell her everything
And she will make it all go away.

I never got the chance to tell her.
She only stayed for one school year.

Objects

There were many fights.
Many arguments.
I would go to my room and close the door.
It was hard to escape in a small apartment.
One thing I knew was that
I did not want my sister to be involved.
The one fight that separated them for that short time,
And I thought it was the last,
Occurred at night.
It was boisterous
Scary
Nerve-wracking
And I thought this was the end.
For all of us.
I put the music on loud in my room.
Avoiding the screams that were scaring my sister.
I listened through the door.
Trying to hear when it was safe to come out.
They were in the living room.
Objects were being thrown.
I grabbed ahold of my sister and told her to be quiet.
We walked down the hallway and passed the living room.
We went unnoticed.
Even though the front door was in their view.
I opened the door
Picked her up
And ran down the stairs.
Where was I going to go?
I took her far away so she couldn't hear the screaming.

It was dark
Late
And we were two kids on the city streets.
I could still see the apartment.
Windows facing the front of the building.
I pretended we were playing a game.
A game she could not understand why it needed to be played
outdoors.
She started to cry.
Suspicious of our exit.
I looked over to the building and saw someone exit.
It was him.
After a few minutes our mother appeared.
Worried.
Wondering where we were.
We came out of hiding and walked over toward her.
She was crying.
Upset.
Yelling at us for leaving.
I didn't know at the time,
But her anger was displaced.
We went back upstairs into the apartment.
We had to clean up the objects.

Menstruation
A time in a girl's life that raises a lot of questions.
The talk.
The informative books.
The secret emergency stash in your backpack.
Most girls are unhappy with this mature change in their lives.
I was one girl who at first
Was relieved.
The day that it first came

I was 12.
I called my mom and told her that I think I got my period.
Did I?
I thought maybe I didn't wipe well after pooping.
Impossible.
She told me to wrap my underwear in a plastic bag
And leave it for her to check.
Bingo.
She was right.
I was becoming a woman.
When *he* got me alone one day
He asked
Did you get your period? Your mom told me.
Finally.
A way out.
This could be the reason why he stops.
I would tell him I have my period.
But then he said
I just have to be more careful.
You can't get pregnant.
It was a part of my life I did not even think about.
Pregnant?
What does this all mean?
It meant fighting harder
Physically
I was getting bigger in size
I was strong
But hormones were stronger.
My breasts increased in size
My butt was larger
His temper was the largest.
The more I fought,
The more aggressive he became.

I was in my room one day
When he approached me.
I would tell him I have my period.
Make snide remarks like
You don't want me to get pregnant, now do you?
A mistake of words I immediately regretted.
He tore off my pants.
I yelped.
No one around.
He bent me over.
This was the first time
He had entered from behind.
There's no way I can get pregnant this way.
I cried.
Pain.
Anguished.
I hated him.
I hated myself even more.
I started to act out.
Missing school.
But always stayed home after everyone in the house left for work.
Being a scholar student was always important to me.
The only thing I had control over.
My future.
I will start my life one day.
Just not today.

Tight Jeans

I stared at the detective taking notes.
Was there any bleeding after the incident?
Why would he ask that question?
Why does it matter now?

This was years ago.
The detective informed my mother to take me to the emergency room
Rape kit.
We drove to the hospital.
Silently driving in the car.
Sweat started to drip under my arms.
I wondered what they were going to think of me
How many girls have they done this on?
I wasn't as nervous about the kit.
Not yet.
I was nervous about all the questions.
More questions
Which requires answers.
More talking.
I wanted to crawl inside my own body and never come out.
I sat in the waiting area of the emergency room.
We went to a hospital where we could not be recognized.
The nurse ushered me into a room.
More questions.
She wanted to know every area that was touched.
That was violated.
When?
How?
How often?
Stop
The questions.
The nurse informed me that there were going to be
Two other physicians in the room.
A male physician.
A female physician.
A nurse.
My mom was allowed to stay in the room with me.

She held onto my hand the entire time.
Tears in her eyes.
I changed into a gown.
They directed me to lie on the table.
I closed my eyes.
They scanned every inch of my body.
They used a light.
They talked among themselves.
Sweat.
Dripping.
Everywhere.
Years later
I would have surgery to battle the sweating issue.
The last part of the kit
Was taking samples.
In areas that I did not want them to explore.
They raised my legs on the stirrups.
Asked me to relax.
How can anyone relax at a time like this?
They inserted the tools they needed to collect any specimen.
I flinched.
And squirmed.
This was not like a regular gyno checkup.
I started to cry.
My mom started to cry.
This was a nightmare.
The male doctor looked over at me and asked
Do you wear jeans?
I thought that was a peculiar question to ask.
Yes.
He looked over at the female physicians.
*It looks like these marks could be from wearing her jeans too
tight.*

Savior

My mom and I packed my bags.
I was getting ready to leave the state.
I started to dream of a new life.
Far away from here.
I would go across the country with my uncle.
Start a new school
And my mom would join me with my sister later.
She needed to find a new job.
We would stay with my uncle for a while
Until we found a place of our own.
I didn't want to leave my friends or my family
But I knew it was best for us.
We would be in hiding.
Far away from *him*.
My mom would fight for full custody of my sister.
After the events unfolded from the night I hit my cousin in
the face
I didn't think I would be here.
I didn't think I would ever break free.
I knew I still wasn't free.
There was still more secrets.
How was I supposed to tell them now?
My mom was dealing with
Detectives
Weddings and
Funerals.
We finally got the phone call.
My cousin had died.
It has been three weeks.
A few days shy of my mother's wedding
To *him*.
I could not bear the lies

My mother had to tell the wedding guests
About why the wedding was canceled.
The death helped as a cover-up.
My uncle had stayed with us a little longer.
To protect us.
Like he said that day.
The day we put spam on my cousin's face.
After I yelled,
Mom, she's crying!
My mother followed me into my room.
Screaming at me
For what I did to my cousin.
For what I said about my grandmother.
I couldn't take it anymore.
No one was listening to me.
But how could they if I never said anything?
My uncle came in the room and tried to keep the peace.
He told my mother to calm down and looked at me.
I told them no one ever listens to me.
No one ever hears my side of the story.
No one protects me.
Protects me?
I could see the looks on their faces.
What did anything have to do with protection?
I became silent.
Nothing.
No words.
Blank stares.
They looked at each other.
Puzzled.
They started firing questions at me.
One
By

One.
My head was spinning.
It's now or never.
At some point during the questioning
It was asked
Is somebody hurting you? Tell me!
I didn't say a word.
COWARD.
I still could not bring the words from my head
To my lips
And say the very words
That should stop the abuse from happening.
More questions.
This time, it was names.
They went through male names
Of people in the family.
It was almost as if they started with
The men who were older.
There weren't many names to go through and
When they stopped at *his* name
I froze.
I didn't say a word.
They now knew.
More questions.
What did he do to you? Tell me! Did he hurt you? Did he
touch you?
What was I supposed to say?
Yes, the very man that you are about to marry in a few weeks
has been sexually abusing me for YEARS.
Not only has he been touching me
but he has been
verbally and
physically abusing me.

He has threatened me with your lives.
The very lives that are now in danger.
The only positive thing I could think about at that moment was
the fact
That my uncle was there.
He was my savior.
But I could not help but think that I might have put his life
In danger too.
What would *he* do?
Are we all dead now?
My mom got up from her chair and
Left the room.
She went into her bedroom
And started cursing him out.
Asking him if it was true.
To this day
I still do not know if he admitted it or not
I still do not know if he said
Yes
Or said
No
Or said anything at all.
My uncle got up from his seat and
Left me in my room
To check on my mom.
She was yelling.
My uncle was yelling.
I started to panic.
I took my jacket and left the apartment.
I ran down the stairs like I did
When they fought years ago.
This time
I did not have anyone with me.

I got outside.
Cool, crisp fall air.
It was dark.
I started to run down the street.
Where am I going?
Who will take me in this late at night?
I had no cell phone.
Only a beeper.
I turned around when I heard yelling.
Was it *him*?
Is this the moment I die?
It was my uncle.
He was yelling at me to come back.
I told him I was never going back there.
He told me he threw *him* out of the house
And he is not coming back.
I said
I didn't believe him.
We walked.
And walked.
And walked.
My uncle asked me questions.
Questions I did not want to answer.
I wanted every secret to stay in my head.
It was louder out here.
My uncle told me to tell him everything
Because he will have his old boys go back
And take care of him.
I pleaded with him.
I did not want him to go back into any of those places
That brought him down.
The drugs.
The stabbing.

The police.
He was now sober
And has been for years.
I was not going to be his breaking point.
HE was not worth it.
The night ended when we stayed over a female friend's house
across the city.
I needed to sleep.
Tomorrow was another day.

Weekend Getaway
My mother received a phone call from
The detective.
He instructed her to stay put in the state.
Challenged our decision to move across the country.
He said that if I was going to
Stand trial
Then I would have to fly back and forth
And it would become expensive
And I would miss school.
It was my freshman year of high school.
We unpacked my bags and stayed throughout the
Investigation.
I had to stay in the apartment.
Scared.
Worried,
Always looking over my shoulder.
Would he return?
Would my family be dead when I arrived home from school?
These thoughts ran through my head daily.
I wrote in my notebook.
Poems.
An escape from the world.

I stopped writing in my journal.
For now.
I knew that things were going to change
But I just didn't know how.
The detectives on the case asked me
If I wanted to stand trial.
Stand trial?
As in answer more questions?
I did not want to stand trial.
I did not want to speak in front of the grand jury.
I did not want to face *him*.
Ever again.
This was a mistake I later regretted.
After witnessing so many survivors
Of sexual assault, abuse, and rape
Who had the courage to stand up to their
Perpetrator
I could not bear to stand trial.
The trial went on without me.
Using statements that were given to the police.
The samples that were provided from the rape kit.
He lost his job.
One that he had for decades.
He was a registered sex offender.
He received weekends **only** in jail.
Yes, you read that right.
He would leave work on a Friday and
Go to jail for the weekend.
Released on Sunday
So he can go to work for the week
Only to do it again
And again
And again

For an abuse that occurred over 6 years and
Serve **three** months of jail time.

Others
The first time I was admitted to a
Psychiatric hospital
My mother could not understand.
What was wrong with me?
Why would I try to kill myself and
Drive my family off the road
If I wasn't being abused anymore?
The culprit was removed from our life.
We started a new one together.
We moved an hour away from where we had lived.
The past was behind us.
But I knew it wasn't.
Secrets.
More I wanted to die with.
My boyfriend at the time knew my secret.
It was something I could hold over him.
What I didn't expect was him to tell my mom.
My boyfriend didn't know the exact details.
But it was enough for my mom to figure out.
During a visit at the psych ward
She looked straight into my eyes.
Moving them side to side
As she always does before she is
About to cry.
She flat-out told me she knew.
She knew I was still being abused.
She knew who it was.
She said *his#2's* name.
How did she know?

She truly didn't.
It was a bluff.
But she was right.
It turns out my great uncle had touched
My sister.
She said it only happened once.
It was enough information for her to
Approach me.
There were more questions.
More for me to answer.
It would be 13 months after my last revelation
Which led me here.

Grooming
Before I started kindergarten
I spent time living at my great grandparents' house.
They owned a two family home
Where my great aunt and great uncle lived
Downstairs.
I was the oldest grandchild and so I was always
Around the adults.
One time it was only me and *him#2*.
He asked me if I knew what a penis was
And if I ever saw one.
I did not know.
I was barely five.
He took his penis out and told me that's what it
Looked like.
He told me it also tasted good.
He pressed his penis against my mouth.
Told me to lick it.
He flopped it back and forth in front of me.
Afterward

He gave me money.
Told me to not tell anyone and
He would give me more.
This became a recurring event.
I didn't think anything was wrong
Until I was older.
He #2 was always nicer to me.
It was our secret.
He never yelled.
Was never aggressive.
Was never mean to me.
He would ask me to help him fix "things"
In the attic.
The attic became a space where
My cousins and I would play so
We were always there.
He would come up and ask me
To help him get something out of the crawl space.
I would follow.
He would pull my pants down and take advantage of me.
I would spend a lot of time
In their new house
Because my mom would drop us off
Every week
While she was taking night classes
For college.
I knew what was going to happen.
Always.
And I often wondered why the adults never
Looked for me.
Why didn't anyone come and rescue me?
As I got older
I would avoid the attic.

Play outside.
Tell my mom I didn't want to play with my cousins.
I asked if they could come over to our house.
Come and play with my toys.
I tried making plans
Every weekend.
Every chance I got to get away.
If someone was staying over at my house then
There was no way I could be abused.
Neither by *him* nor *him#2*.
I would be saved.
For at least one more day.
No more grooming.

Screen Door

Shortly before my first stay at the psychiatric hospital
My great aunt and great uncle came
To our new place for a visit.
He#2 told my mom that he would go to the hardware store
With me since I knew my way around the new neighborhood.
I got in his car.
Knowing what he wanted to do to me.
We drove around the winding roads.
I looked straight ahead.
His right hand reached over
And he placed it in between my pants.
I told him to stop.
He looked puzzled.
He asked me what *he* did to me and if any of it
Was as good as what *he* #2 did to me.
I shoved his hand away and
Told him to keep his hands on the wheel.
We went inside the hardware store and purchased

The items my mom requested.
On the drive home
He attempted to put his hand between my legs again.
He said he will get to me and it was only a matter of time.
I told him that he was done and to watch out
Before he ended up like *him*.
He didn't appreciate that response.
The car stopped outside my house and before he could grab me
I opened the screen door, which was broken.
The reason why we went to the hardware store.
The corner of the door slammed into the inner side of my
ankle.
It bled.
A lot.
A scar would form and be with me forever.
A scar that tells a story of the first time I stood up for myself.
A scar that would prove it was the last time I would be
Taken advantage of.
A scar that I would later place a tattoo over to
Not be reminded of that day again.

Nightmares

Have always played a major role in my life.
A role that I would have to battle with
The unconscious mind.
There are dreams where
People are chasing me
I am falling down a hole
People I care dearly for are dead
Times where I am trying to fight and
My arms are moving slow.
One thing my experience cannot take away
From me

Is my day.
I am learning to control every part of my life.
One where I have to battle with the mental illness
And turmoil it has placed on my consciousness.
Writing this book has been an outlet for my past.
A past that is decades gone.
Forever.

AFTERWORD

It was Friday the 13th, 2020. The lockdown. The pandemic. Gas prices were under $1.89. School buildings were shut down for months. All nonessential stores and businesses were mandated to close. Sporting events, parks, trails, church, concerts, festivals, weddings, and holiday gatherings all canceled. My new dystopian world became an avenue for writing my story. People began to purge items from their homes. The place they had ignored while spending time at work, school, or any other activities outside the house. After months of being forced to stare at the same four walls, I began to declutter. What was the purpose of keeping old letters? Old journals? I have moved from place to place and traveled with the same dusty bins. Only to hide them in a new location. The truth is, I wanted to read every letter. Every entry. Before tossing them away. At the same time, I needed security, safety, and a plan. After contacting a therapist who I would see virtually, the plan started to fall into place. Week by week, we started reading each letter and then each journal. I set a goal of writing 10 pages a week. A target that I often failed. I needed time to process every bit of information. Gather my thoughts. Create a structure. Heal the open wounds. It became a drug to me. One that I couldn't wait to kick the habit. My late stepfather once asked me, "Why do you want to open old wounds?" I have thought about this question a lot. It wasn't until after he passed away that I realized my wounds had never healed. As each and every one of us gets older, we digest wisdom and experience life through a new lens. It is vital to process your own history at a time when your mind has the energy to repair things. I offer this story as a tactic for you to search for an approach in self-healing. For decades, I swore I would bury my story in the ground with me. But I aspire to be cremated and therefore cannot have any fuel to burn.

ABOUT THE AUTHOR

Agatha Sicil was born in New York City. She is a graduate of Pace University, and received her M.A. from Mercy College before returning to Pace University where she received an M.A.T.. She is a full-time special education teacher and a part-time writer. Agatha is the author of many works including "Burn," the prologue to her creative nonfiction piece, "Before You Met Me." She lives in the New England region with her husband and children.

You can visit Agatha Sicil at https://www.agathasicil.com and follow her on Twitter @agathasicil and on Instagram @read_a-gathasicil

RIZE publishes great stories and great writing across genres written by those from underrepresented groups. Our team consists of:

Lisa Diane Kastner, Founder and Executive Editor
Rebecca Dimyan, Editor
Andrew DiPrinzio, Editor
Cecilia Kennedy, Editor
Barbara Lockwood, Editor
Cody Sisco, Editor
Chih Wang, Editor
Benjamin White, Editor
Peter A. Wright, Editor
Pulp Art Studios, Cover Design
Standout Books, Interior Design
Polgarus Studios, Interior Design
Nicole Tiskus, Production Manager
Alex Riklin, Production Manager
Alexis August, Production Manager
Joelle Mitchell, Head of Licensing
Lara Macaaione, Director of Marketing
Pulp Art Studios, Cover Design
Standout Books, Interior Design
Polgarus Studios, Interior Design

Learn more about us and our stories at www.runningwildpress.com/rize

Loved this story and want more? Follow us at www.running-wildpress.com/rize, www.facebook/rize, on Twitter @rizerwp and Instagram @rizepress